Scholastic Phonics

Fantastic Skeletons

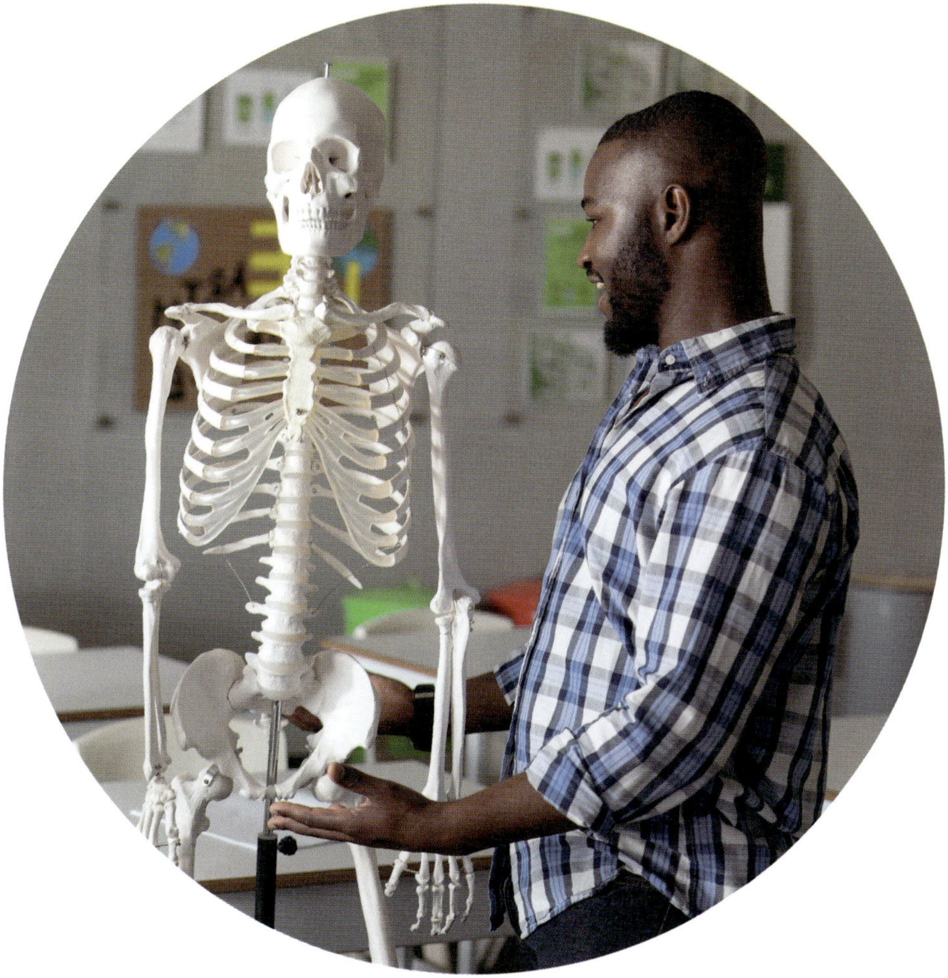

Published in the UK by Scholastic Education, 2023
Scholastic Distribution Centre, Bosworth Avenue, Tournament Fields, Warwick, CV34 6UQ
Scholastic Ireland, 89E Lagan Road, Dublin Industrial Estate, Glasnevin, Dublin, D11 HP5F

SCHOLASTIC and associated logos are trademarks and/or registered trademarks of Scholastic Inc.
www.scholastic.co.uk
© 2023 Scholastic
1 2 3 4 5 6 7 8 9   3 4 5 6 7 8 9 0 1 2

Printed by Ashford Colour Press
The book is made of materials from well-managed, FSC®-certified forests and other controlled sources.

A CIP catalogue record for this book is available from the British Library.
ISBN 978-0702-32110-8

All rights reserved. This book is sold subject to the condition that it shall not, by way of trade or otherwise, be lent, hired out or otherwise circulated in any form of binding or cover other than that in which it is published. No part of this publication may be reproduced, stored in a retrieval system, or transmitted in any form or by any other means (electronic, mechanical, photocopying, recording or otherwise) without prior written permission of Scholastic.

Every effort has been made to trace copyright holders for the works reproduced in this publication, and the publishers apologise for any inadvertent omissions.

Author
Ann Hill

Editorial team
Rachel Morgan, Vicki Yates, Abbie Rushton, Jennie Clifford

Design team
Dipa Mistry, Andrea Lewis, We Are Grace

Photographs
Cover ledwell/iStock
p1, 3, 4–5, 9 wavebreakmedia/Shutterstock
p6 stocksolutions/Shutterstock
p7 PinkCoffee Studio/Shutterstock
p8 Robert Kneschke/Shutterstock
p10, 24 Sergey Novikov/Shutterstock
p11 Twinsterphoto/Shutterstock
p12 Soloviova Liudmyla/Shutterstock
p13 Kotin/Shutterstock
p14 Felix Mizioznikov/Shutterstock
p15 T.Photo/Shutterstock
p16 Puwadol Jaturawutthichai/Shutterstock
p17 FatCamera/iStock
p18 (green leafy veg) Svetlana Lukienko/Shutterstock
p18 (bread) Elena Zajchikova
p18 (cheese and milk) nehopelon/iStock
p19 Manny DaCunha/Shutterstock
p20, 24 FOTOGRIN/Shutterstock
p21 (mouse) Rudmer Zwerver/Shutterstock
p21 (mouse skeleton) 3drenderings/Shutterstock
p22, 24 annop youngrot/Shutterstock
p23 RealityImages/Shutterstock

Help your child to read!

This book practises these letters and letter sounds.
Point and say the sounds with your child:

- y (as in 'body')
- ea (as in 'healthy')
- ow (as in 'grow')
- g (as in 'fragile')
- ph (as in 'elephant')
- le (as in 'flexible')
- ve (as in 'active')
- se (as in 'mouse')
- ou (as in 'you')

Your child may need help to read these common tricky words:

of, are, the, would, our, to, all, your, they, do, one, what

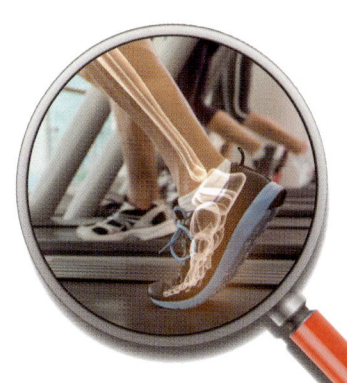

Before reading
- Look at the cover picture and read the title together. Read the back cover blurb to your child.
- Ask your child: *Have you learned about skeletons or bones before? What are they?*
- Talk about the image in the magnifying glass.

During reading
- If your child gets stuck on a word, remind them to sound it out and then blend the sounds to read the word: m-ou-l-t-s, moults.
- If they are still stuck, show them how to read the word.
- Enjoy looking at the pictures together. Pause to talk about the information.

After reading
- Talk about the images on page 24. What can your child tell you about them?
- Ask your child: *How many bones are in your skeleton? Which part keeps your brain safe?*
- Discuss which bones are the most useful, and why.

An adult skeleton is made up of 206 bones. Some bones are long, like leg bones. Others are tiny, like those in the hands, feet and toes.

Without a skeleton, we would collapse!

The skull keeps the fragile brain safe.

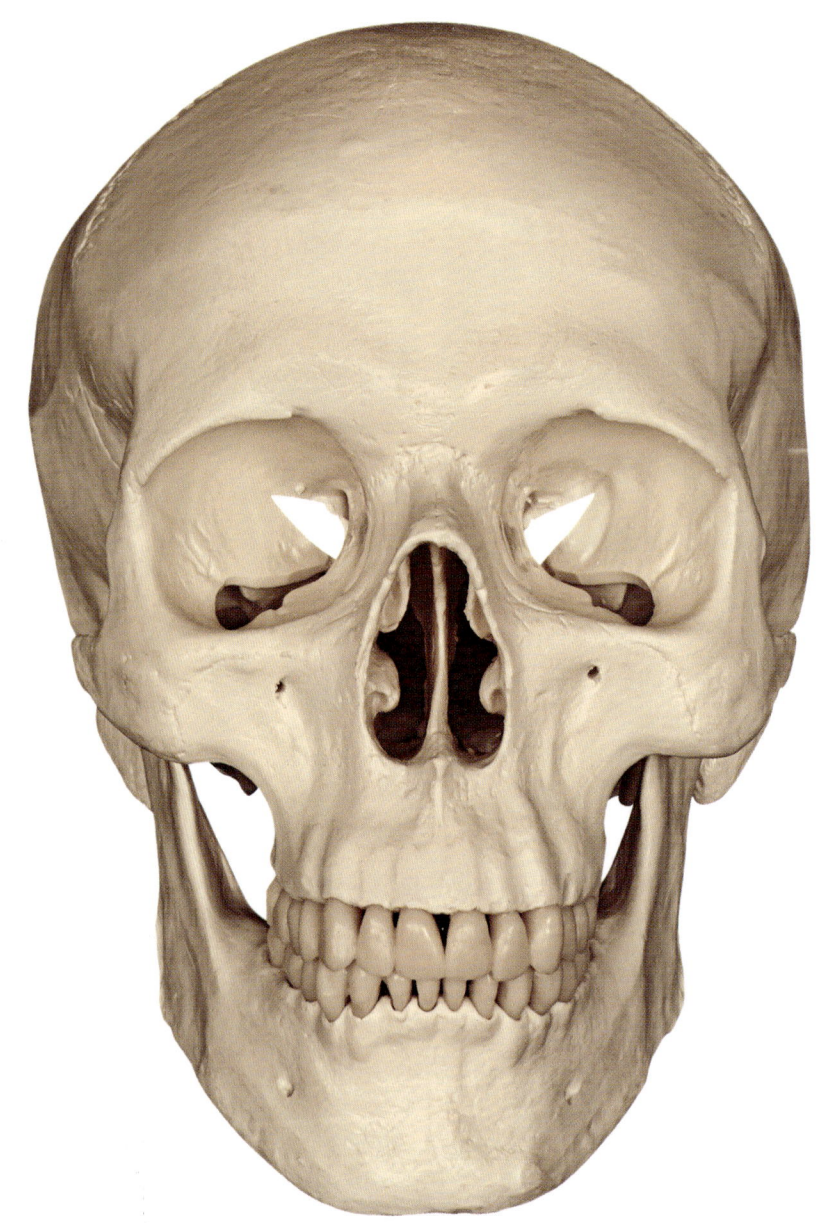

The front of the nose is made from softer tissue than bone.

The bones in our skeletons are connected so that we can run, bend and balance.

Spreading our arms helps us to balance.

Groups of little bones in the feet make them flexible.

9

Bones meet in places like the elbow, neck and all down the back. Elbows let our arms bend.

The elbow and shoulder help us raise a hand.

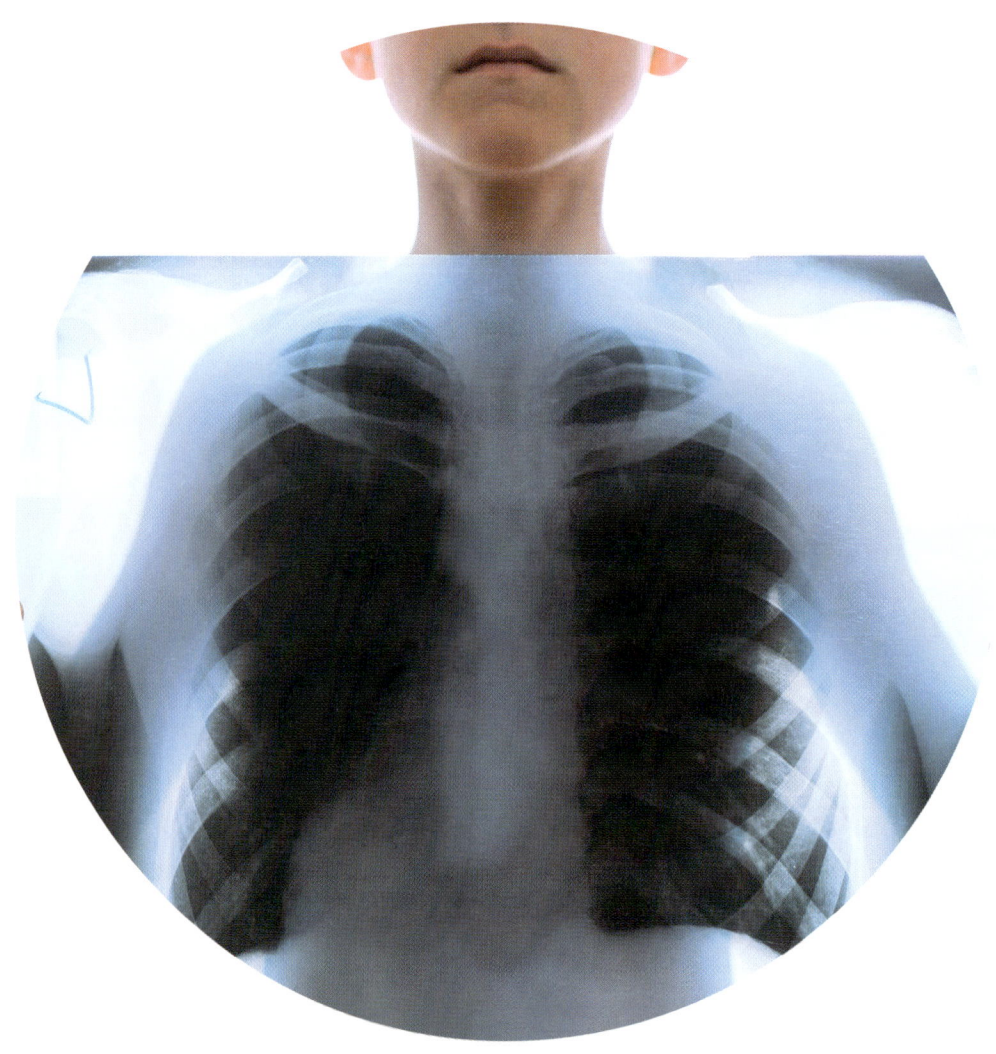

A group of bones makes up the ribcage. The ribcage keeps fragile parts of the body safe.

Touch the middle of your chest and you will feel the breastbone.

ribcage

breastbone

Bones are not made from rubber so they do not bounce!

A bone might crack if you tumble.

Some things help to keep bones safe when you are active.

helmet

pads

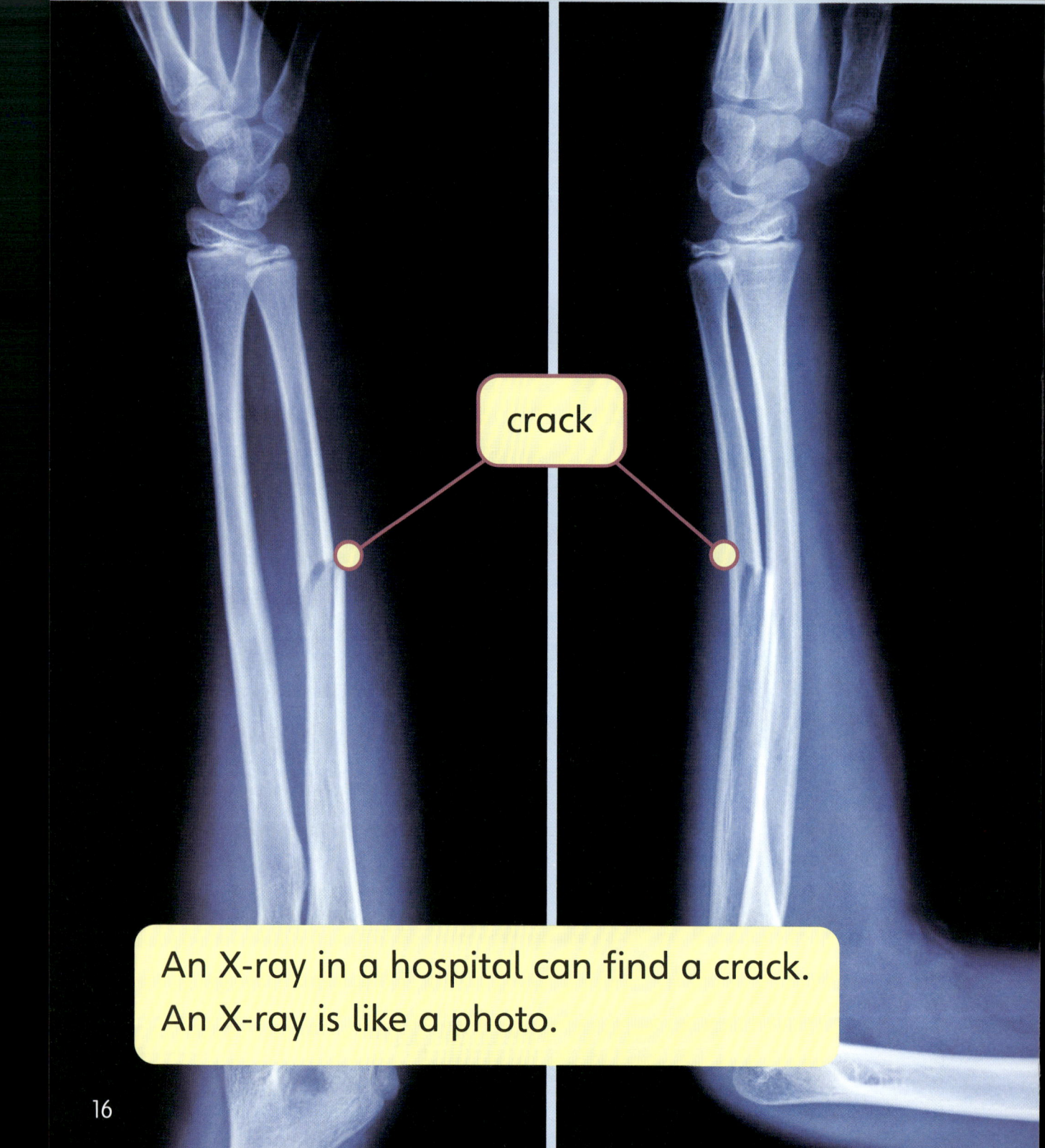

crack

An X-ray in a hospital can find a crack.
An X-ray is like a photo.

Bones must be protected until they are fixed. They heal in one to three months.

Eating these healthy foods helps bones to grow:
- cheese and milk
- green leafy veg
- beans
- some breads
- fish.

Exercise strengthens bones, too.

Most animals have skeletons – from a giant elephant to a tiny mouse!

African elephant

Elephants are heavy so need strong leg bones.

A little mouse has at least 225 bones.

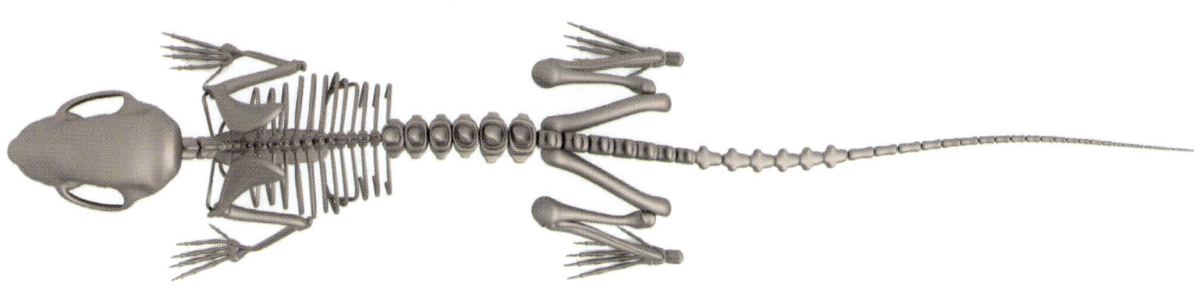

What sort of skeletons have a fly and a spider got?

house fly

They have hard outer skeletons.

To grow, a spider moults (sheds its skeleton). A bigger skeleton takes its place.

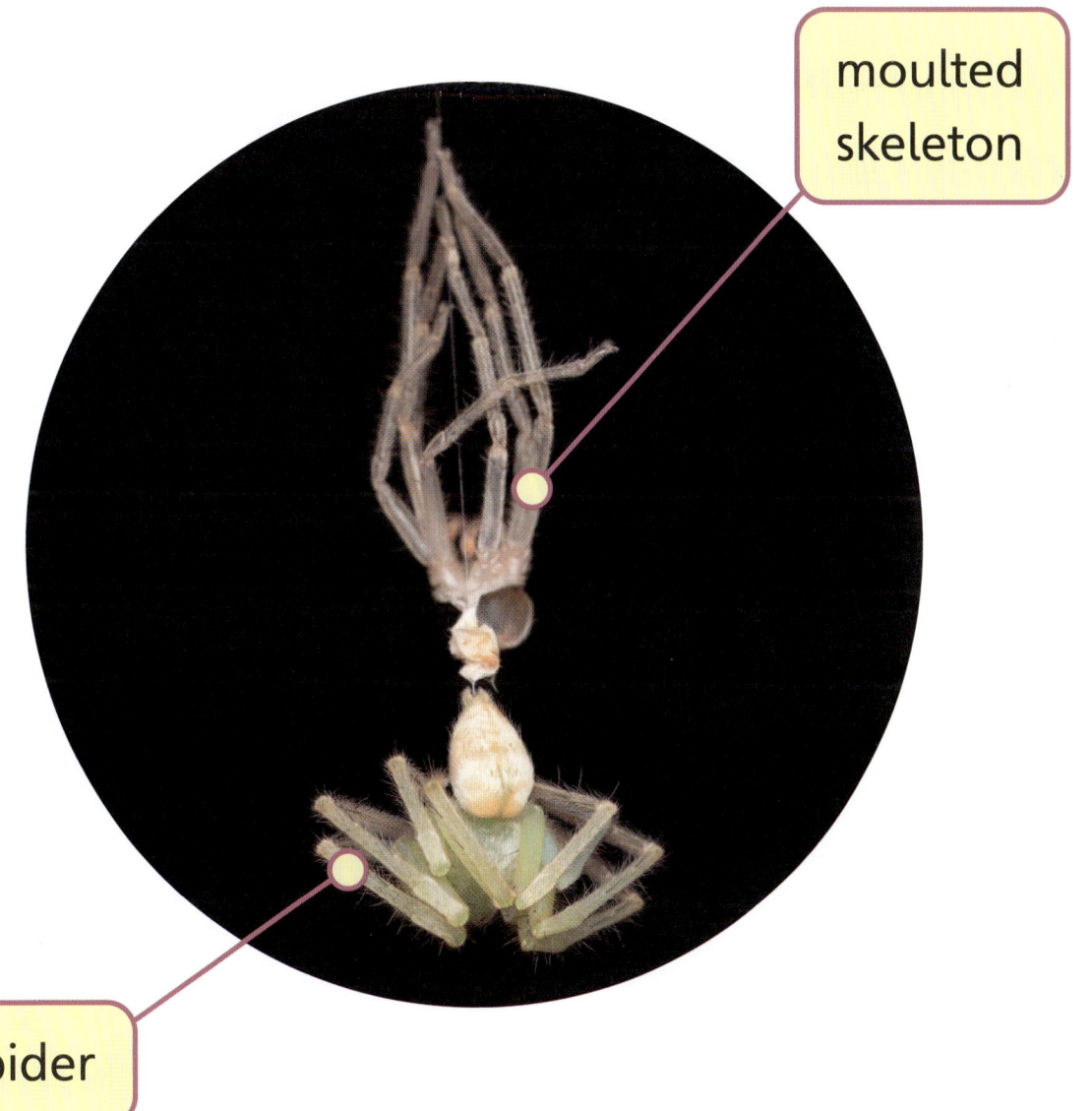

moulted skeleton

spider

Talk about it!